PINT

RECIPES

By: Sue McNair

Sue McNair

ISBN: 147527470X
ISBN-13: 9781475274707

DEDICATION

This book is dedicated to anyone who enjoys bettering themselves in the kitchen.

CONTENTS

56. Extra Easy Coffee Cake
57. Extra Easy Lasagna
58. Fast And Easy Pizza
59. Graham Cracker Quickie
60. Greek style potato salad
61. Honey Butter
62. Light And Easy Lasagna
63. Light And Easy Picante Fish (microwave)
64. Longhorn Quick Chili Dip
65. Make-it-easy Beef Potpie
66. Pasta Susanna
67. Quick And Chewy Chocolate Drops
68. Quick And Comfy Macaroni And Cheese
69. Quick And Creamy Applesauce Dessert
70. Quick And Dirty Yucatan Tacos
71. Quick And Easy Chocolate Brownies
72. Quick And Easy Fudgey Brownies
73. Quick And Easy Lemon Cheesecake
74. Quick and Easy Mexican Bean Soup
75. Quick And Easy Pumpkin Bread
76. Quick And Easy Pumpkin Pie
77. Quick And Easy Shortbread
78. Quick And Easy Tarragon Chicken
79. Quick And Easy Vanilla Ice Cream
80. Quick And Easy Waffles
81. Quick And Sassy Cocktail Bites
82. Quick And Simple Pasta Salad
83. Quick And Spicy Beans
84. Quick And Spicy Chicken And Rice
85. Quick Apple Muffins
86. Quick Apple Sauce
87. Quick Baked Pasta Family Style
88. Quick Barbecue Beef Bake
89. Quick Barbecue Sauce
90. Quick Bean and Cheese Enchiladas
91. Quick Beef And Cheese Burritos
92. Quick Beef Casserole
93. Quick Beef Minestrone
94. Quick Beef Pie
95. Quick Beef Sausage
96. Quick Beef Stew
97. Quick Biscuit Mix
98. Quick Biscuits
99. Quick Blueberry Muffins
100. Quick Bread Sticks
101. Quick Broccoli And Rice Casserole

ACKNOWLEDGMENTS

Thanks to everyone currently sharing recipes around
the world

A Quick Dessert

Ingredients:

4 Pieces toast

4 slices cheese

Nutmeg

1 1/2 c Applesauce

1/4 c Sugar

Directions:

Add sugar and nutmeg to applesauce. Put applesauce on toast, about 3 tablespoons on each piece of toast. Lay a slice of cheese over the sauce. Bake in a moderate oven until the cheese melts. Serve hot.

A Quick Way To Decorate Cake

Ingredients:

1 pk Marshmallows

Vanilla to taste

Green food coloring

1 pk Red hots

Box of cornflakes (4 1/2 c)

White angel food cake

Directions:

Melt marshmallows, add food coloring and vanilla. Add the cornflakes, stir until well coated. Spread this onto a cookie sheet, shaping into holly leaves. Place a red hot in middle. Let dry about 5 hours. Then top a white frosted angel cake with the holly leaves. Makes a very pretty cake.

A Real Easy Cookie

Ingredients:

Graham crackers

Pecan halves

1/2 c Sugar

2 Sticks cutter

Directions:

Melt butter and sugar. Bring to a boil. Boil for two minutes ONLY. Place graham crackers on foil lined sheet. Place nuts on cracker center. Spoon butter and sugar mix over graham crackers. Bake at 325 degrees for 15 minutes on top rack. Cool completely before breaking apart.

Baked Mac And Cheese

Ingredients:

1 cn (10 3/4 ounces) Condensed Cheddar Cheese Soup

1/2 cn Milk

1 ts Prepared Mustard

1/8 ts Pepper

2 c Hot cooked Elbow or medium shell Macaroni (1 1/2 c dry)

2 ts Margarine or Butter, melted

1 tb Dry Bread Crumbs

Directions:

In 1-quart casserole, combine soup, milk, mustard and pepper. Stir in macaroni.

In a cup, combine margarine and bread crumbs. Sprinkle over casserole.

Bake at 400 degrees F. 20 minutes or until hot and bubbling.

Makes 2 1/2 Cups = 2 main dish servings or 4 side dish servings.

Beef and Rice Crisp

Ingredients:

1 lb Lean ground beef

1 c Coarsely-chopped onion

1/2 c Coarsely-chopped green pepper

2 tb Ketchup

1/4 ts Salt

1/2 ts Dry mustard

1 1/2 c Cooked rice

1 c Milk

1 (10 oz) can cream of Mushroom soup

1 1/2 c Shredded Cheddar cheese

1 ts Worcestershire sauce

2 c Corn flakes, coarsely crushed

3 tb Butter, melted

Directions:

Saute beef, onion and green pepper in a large fry pan until meat is browned; drain off any fat. Blend in ketchup, salt and dry mustard. Turn meat mixture into a 2 quart round casserole; spread rice on top. Gradually stir milk into mushroom soup. Stir in cheese and Worcestershire sauce. Pour over meat and rice layers. Combine crushed corn flakes and butter; sprinkle evenly over casserole. Bake in preheated 375 degree F oven 35 to 40 minutes or until hot and bubbly. Makes 6 servings.

Beef And Scallop Saute

Ingredients:

2 tb Peanut oil

1 ts Minced garlic

1 lb Beef cut for stir fry

1 pn Red pepper flakes

3/4 lb Sea scallops

1 pn Red pepper flakes

1 1/4 c Sliced green onion

1 tb Water

1 pn Fresh ginger

1 pn White pepper

1 ts Salt

Directions:

Heat oil in wok or large skillet until almost smoking. Add garlic and beef, then scallops, and stir-fry about 30 seconds. Add remaining ingredients and stir-fry beef and scallops another 20 to 30 seconds.

Berry Easy Barbecue Sauce

Ingredients:

18 oz Barbecue sauce

16 oz Cranberry sauce, jellied

1/4 c Water

2 tb Brown sugar, packed

2 tb Chili powder

1/4 ts Garlic powder

1/4 ts Cloves, ground

Directions:

Combine all the ingredients in a 2 quart saucepan. Bring to boiling; reduce heat and simmer for 10 minutes.

Brush on meat or chicken at end of grilling time.

Makes 3 1/2 cups of sauce - enough for 18 - 21 pounds of ribs.

Cheap And Easy Bean And Hominy Stew

Ingredients:

1 cn Hominy, canned

1 cn Pinto beans

1 cn Garbanzo beans

1 cn Kidney beans

6 oz Tomato sauce

1 pk Chili/taco/mexican seasoning

Directions:

Mix and heat.

Easy Apple Relish

Ingredients:

2 c Fresh cranberries

2 x Apples

Orange, peeled and seeded

2 c Sugar

Directions:

Finely chop (or grind) cranberries, apples and orange. Mix with sugar and refrigerate for a day or two before serving. Great with chicken or turkey.

Easy Banana Nut Bread

Ingredients:

1/2 c Butter

1 c Sugar

2 Eggs

4 sm Bananas, mashed

3/4 ts Baking soda

1/2 ts Salt

1 1/2 c Flour

3/4 c Chopped walnuts

Directions:

Cream butter and sugar until fluffy; add eggs one at a time beating well after each addition. Stir in bananas.

Add dry ingredients and mix well. Pour into bread pan, bake at 350F for 30-35 minutes.

Easy Banana Smores For Kids

Ingredients:

2 Bananas; sliced

2 Flat chocolate bars

2 Small jars marshmallow fluff

Nabisco Honey Maid Grahams

Directions:

Put 2 bananas slices on a graham cracker, add a square of chocolate and a large spoonful of marshmallow fluff. Put another graham cracker on top and squish together.

Easy Barbecued Chicken Casserole

Ingredients:

1 cn Pork and beans (16oz)

4 Chicken pieces

1/4 c Catsup

2 tb Peach preserves

2 ts Onion, instant minced

1/4 ts Soy sauce

1/4 c Brown sugar

Directions:

Place beans in a 2-quart casserole; top with casserole. Mix together remaining ingredients; pour over chicken and beans.

Cover and bake in preheated 325 deg.F. oven for 1 3/4 hours.

Easy Cheesy Lemon Bars

Ingredients:

1 pk Lemon cake mix

1 Stick of butter, melted

1 Egg

1 pk Lemon frosting mix

2 Eggs

8 oz Cream cheese, softened

Directions:

Mix all ingredients for the cake together; do NOT add any ingredients to the cake mix as per the box instructions. Pat into the bottom of a 13 x 9 pan. Mix together the frosting mix, eggs, and cream cheese. Pour evenly over cake batter and bake at 350F for 40 minutes.

Easy Cherry Cobbler

Ingredients:

1 cn 21-oz. cherry pie filling

1/2 ts Almond extract

1/2 pk 18-oz. cake mix (about 2 C)

Pecans; chopped, optional

1/4 c To 1/2 cup butter; melted

Directions:

Mix cherry pie filling w/almond extract and pour into buttered 9"x9" pan. Sprinkle cake mix and nuts over pie filling. Drizzle melted butter over all. Bake in a 350 degrees F oven for 55 mins. Serve warm w/ice cream.

Easy Chicken Pastry Bites

Ingredients:

1 cn Crescent Rolls (8 rolls)

1/2 pk Perdue Italian Style Short-Cuts

1 tb Pizza Quick Sauce

Directions:

Separate the 8 crescent roll triangles. Mix the sauce and the chicken, and divide the mixture equally among the triangles. Pinch closed the triangles so that chicken is completely surrounded. Bake for 20 minutes at 375.

Easy Chili

Ingredients:

1 cn Kidney beans

1/2 lb Hamburger

1 cn Tomato soup

1 tb Chili powder

1 sm Onion, chopped

Directions:

Dump all into a pot. Bring to a boil. Turn down and simmer about 30 minutes.

Easy Crockpot Barbecue

Ingredients:

3 lb Pork roast; (up to 4)

1 lg Onion

8 Whole cloves; sliced, (up to 10)

Your favorite barbecue sauce

Directions:

Before you go to bed, brown pork roast in skillet with a small amount of oil. Peel and slice 1 large onion. Place 1/2 onion in bottom of crockpot. Put roast in crockpot and add 1/2 to 3/4 cup water. Add rest of onion and cloves. Set on low. In morning, turn off crockpot, remove meat, and let cool. Discard onion and juices in crockpot. Tear roast into small pieces. Put back in crockpot and add barbecue sauce (enough until juicy). Cook on low 2 to 3 hours or until flavors are blended. Serve on buns.

Easy Donuts

Ingredients:

1 1/2 c Flour

1/4 ts Salt

2 ts Baking powder

2/3 c Milk

2 tb Powdered sugar

Directions:

Sift dry ingredients together and add egg and milk, batter will be thick. If too thin add a little more flour. Drop by spoonfuls into deep fat and cook till browned. The powdered sugar is sprinkled on the donuts after they are cooked.

Easy Florentine Rice

Ingredients:

1/2 lb Fresh spinach

1 tb Butter or margarine

1 md Red bell pepper, chopped

1/2 c Sliced green onions

3 cl Garlic, minced

1/4 ts Ground white pepper

1/4 ts Dried whole rosemary, crushed

3 c Cooked rice

1/2 c Freshly grated Parmesan cheese

1/3 c Pine nuts, toasted

Directions:

Remove stems from spinach. Wash leaves thoroughly and tear into large pieces. Melt butter in large skillet over medium-high heat. Add spinach, red bell pepper, onions, garlic, pepper and rosemary. cook for 2 to 3 minutes or until spinach is softened. Stir in rice, cheese and nuts. Stir until thoroughly heated and cheese is melted.

Easy Freezer Strawberry Sorbet

Ingredients:

2 pk Unflavored gelatin

1 c Sugar

3 c Water

1 qt Pureed strawberries about 3 pints fresh

1 c Cranberry juice cocktail

1/4 c Fresh squeezed lemon juice

Directions:

Combine gelatin and sugar in a medium saucepan; stir in water. Let stand 2 minutes. Cook over low heat, stirring constantly until gelatin dissolves. Remove from heat; cool. Stir in strawberry puree and remaining ingredients. Pour into a 13x9 pan. Cover and freeze 8 hours or overnight. Spoon about 1/4 of frozen mixture into the container of a blender or food processor. Top with lid and process until smooth. Return to pan. Repeat until all the mixture has been processed. Return pan to freezer and freeze for 4 hours or until firm. Let stand at room temperature 15-20 minutes before serving.

Easy French Bread

Ingredients:

1 1/2 c Water

3 1/4 c White bread flour

1 1/2 tb Sugar

1 1/2 ts Salt

3 ts Active dry yeast

Directions:

Put all ingredients in bread machine pan. Set for a large loaf. Use regular or rapid bake cycle. To develop the crisp crust that French bread is known for, turn the machine off and reset it after the first knead cycle is completed. This gives the bread extra kneading time and results in a crisp crust.

Easy Fruit Cobbler

Ingredients:

1 cn 21 oz fruit pie filling, any flavor

1 1/4 c Bisquick

1 tb Sugar

1/4 c Milk

1/4 c Sour cream

Directions:

Heat oven to 425 degrees F. Grease 1 1/2 qt casserole. Heat pie filling to boiling. Pour into casserole.

Mix remaining ingredients until dough forms. Drop by 6 spoons full onto hot pie filling. Sprinkle with sugar if desired.

Bake about 20 minutes or until biscuits are golden brown.

Easy Fruit Dessert Cups

Ingredients:

8 oz Can pineapple chunks, drained

1 1/4 c Red seedless grapes

2 Kiwifruit, peeled, sliced

4 lg Scoops Vanilla Ice Cream

1/4 c Orange flavored liqueur (optional)

Directions:

Combine all the fruits; cover and refrigerate.

When ready to serve, spoon fruit mixture into individual dessert dishes. Top with a scoop of ice cream and drizzle a little of the liqueur over ice cream.

Easy Fudge

Ingredients:

3 c Chopped chocolate or chocolate wafers (sweet, semisweet, or a combination)

1 cn Sweetened condensed milk

Pinch of salt

1 ts Vanilla

1/2 c Chopped nuts

Directions:

A very good fudge with no cooking or thermometer watching. Melt chocolate in the top of a double boiler over hot, not boiling water. Remove from heat and stir in remaining ingredients. Spread in a generously buttered 8-inch square pan. Chill 2 hours or until firm. Turn fudge out onto a cutting board, cut into squares. Store in tightly covered containers. Makes 49 pieces.

Easy Fudge 2

Ingredients:

6 tb Margarine

3 1/2 c Confectioners' sugar

1/2 c Sifted cocoa powder

1 ts Vanilla extract

1/4 c Soy milk

1 c Chopped nuts (optional)

Directions:

Lightly grease a 5 x 9-inch loaf pan using a little of the margarine.

Place the remaining margarine, sugar, cocoa, vanilla and soy milk in a heatproof mixing bowl or the upper part of a double boiler.

Place the bowl or boiler over simmering water and stir until smooth. Add the nuts if desired.

Pour the mixture quickly into the prepared pan. Chill thoroughly and cut into squares.

Makes 2 to 3 dozen squares

Sue McNair

Easy Graham Cracker Cookies

Ingredients:

24 Graham crackers, separated in half

1 c Butter

1 c Brown sugar

1 c Chopped walnuts

Directions:

Preheat oven to 350 degrees F. Use a cookie sheet with sides. Place crackers on cookie sheet. In a small sauce pan, heat butter and sugar until boiling. Add nuts to mixture. Pour over crackers. bake 10 minutes

Easy Hodge Podge Soup

Ingredients:

1 lb Hamburger

1 Chopped onion

Salt and pepper

1 cn (10.75-oz) tomato soup

1 cn (16-oz) mixed vegetables

1 cn (16-oz) kidney beans

1 Box (14.75-oz) spaghetti

Directions:

Brown hamburger and onions. Drain excess grease. Add tomato soup and half a can of water. Stir in vegetables. Run knife through spaghetti to cut strands. Add to soup mixture. Bring to boil, simmer 15 minutes.

Easy Hot Dog Cheese Roll Ups

Ingredients:

30 Cocktail franks

10 Cheese slices

2 pk Crecent rolls

Directions:

Take the roll dough and unroll them carefully. Cut each triangle in half. (will need part of the second box; but not all) ; keeping the triangular shape. Then wrap 1/3 or a piece of cheese around the frank and holding it with your fingers start rolling it in the roll. Start at the large end of the triangle and roll towards the tip. Bake in a hot oven until brown...should only take about 10 minutes at 400 degrees. Watch carefully. Take out when they are browned. Serve immediately.

Easy Hungarian Soup

Ingredients:

2 lb Stewing beef

3 tb Butter

1 Onion, chopped

1 Clove garlic, minced

1 tb Paprika

2 cn (10 3/4 oz) tomato soup

9 c Water

1/4 ts Caraway seeds

4 md Carrots, sliced

4 oz Wide noodles

10 oz Frozen cut green beans

1 c Sour cream

Directions:

Using large soup kettle, brown beef on all sides in butter; remove beef and set aside. Brown onion and garlic in butter until soft, stirring occasionally. Stir in paprika. Return beef to kettle; add soup, water, caraway, and carrots. Bring to a boil; reduce heat, cover and let simmer 45 minutes. Stir in noodles and green beans with soup over high heat. Once soup boils, reduce to simmer, cover and continue cooking about 20 minutes. Stir occasionally. Stir in sour cream until blended. Heat, but do not allow to boil.

Serves 8.

Easy Ice Cream Recipe

Ingredients:

5 Eggs

Pinch of Salt

2 c Sugar

2 pk Instant pudding mix

1 cn Evaporated milk

2 Qt. milk

Directions:

Beat eggs well. add salt. blend in sugar and pudding mix. add milks. stir well. Pour in container, (plastic works best), store in freezer at least over night.

Easy Meatball Paprikash

Ingredients:

1 - lb lean ground pork or veal

1 - large egg

1/4 - cup fine dry bread crumbs

1 - tsp salt

1/2 - tsp caraway seeds

2 - Tbsp vegetable oil

1 - large onion, chopped, about 1 cup

1 - large green bell pepper, cored, seeded and cut into 1" chunks

2 - Tbsp paprika

1 - 16 oz can stewed tomatoes

1 - 8 oz pkg wide egg noodles

Directions:

In large bowl, combine pork, egg, bread crumbs, 1/2 tsp salt and caraway seeds; using hands or wooden spoon, blend well. Shape into 1 1/2" balls. In 12" skillet over medium-high heat, heat oil; add meatballs; cook about 12 minutes, turning frequently until well browned on all sides. Using a slotted spoon, remove meatballs to plate. To drippings in skillet, add onion, green pepper and paprika; cook, still over medium-high heat, 5 minutes, stirring frequently until vegetables are crisp-tender and well coated with paprika. Return meatballs to skillet, along with tomatoes with their liquid and remaining 1/2 tsp salt. Increase heat to high; bring to boil. Reduce heat to low; simmer, covered, 10 minutes, stirring occasionally until meatballs are cooked through. Meanwhile, prepare noodles according to package directions.

To serve: Stir sour cream into meatball mixture; remove from heat. Spoon meatballs into serving platter. Drain noodles; toss with chopped parsley; arrange on platter with meatballs.

Easy Microwave Peanut Butter Fudge

Ingredients:

1 Bag semi-sweet chocolate chips (12 oz)

1 Jar smooth or crunchy peanut butter (12 oz)

1 cn Sweetened condensed milk (14 oz)

Directions:

Makes approximately 42 pieces. In a 1-1/2 quart microwave-proof bowl, melt chocolate and peanut butter on HIGH for 3 minutes. Remove from microwave; stir will. Add milk, stirring until well blended. Pour mixture into 8 x 8 inch pan, lined with waxed paper. Refrigerate to chill.

Easy Microwave Pizza Bagels

Ingredients:

1 Lender's plain bagel

Squeeze pizza sauce

Mozzarella cheese

Directions:

Heat bagel in microwave on high for 15 seconds. Split bagel, add sauce and some cheese. Heat in microwave on high for 30 to 45 seconds or until cheese melts.

Easy Nonfat Garlic Bread

Ingredients:

1 c Oil-free italian dressing

1 ts Paprika

5 Cl Garlic; or more to taste

1 Whole-wheat french bread

Parsley flakes; optional

Directions:

Preheat the broiler. Place the dressing, paprika, and garlic in a blender and process until well blended. Brush this mixture on the bread and sprinkle with parsley, if desired.

Easy Oven Stew

Ingredients:

3/4 lb Boneless beef round steak, trimmed and cubed

1 tb Cooking oil

4 md Potatoes, cut into 1 inch cubes

5 md Carrots, cut into 1 1/2 inch chunks

1 Rib celery, cut into 1 inch chunks

1 lg Onion, cut into 1 inch chunks

14 1/4 oz Can of chunky stewed tomatoes

3 tb Quick cooking tapioca

1 ts Browning sauce

1/4 ts Pepper

1 c Frozen peas

Directions:

In Dutch oven, brown the steak in oil. Add the next eight ingredients; cover and bake at 300 for 4 to 5 hours. Add the peas during the last 30 minutes of baking. Yield: 6 servings

Easy Pasta Speciala

Ingredients:

1 15 oz can stewed tomatoes

1 sm Can Rotel diced

Pepper/tomatoes

1 15 oz can French-cut green beans

1 15 oz can mushrooms stems and pieces

2 tb Italian seasoning

1/2 ts Garlic powder

Directions:

Mix it all together in a big saucepan, bring to a boil and simmer for half hour or so. Serve it over spiral pasta and top with FF parmesan.

Easy Pear Dessert

Ingredients:

1 tb Butter

3 Ripe pears

1/2 c Butterscotch or caramel ice cream topping

Scoops of vanilla ice cream or Ice Milk

Directions:

Peel, core and thinly slice pears.

Heat butter in a medium skillet over medium heat. Add the sliced pears. Cook until pears are softened, stirring occasionally. Add the topping and heat until the mixture is bubbly, stirring occasionally.

Serve over ice cream.

Easy Pork Chop Dinner

Ingredients:

4 Pork chops

Can of chicken broth

1 Onion chopped

2 Cloves of garlic - chopped

2 ts Of olive oil

Directions:

Put oil in frying pan and heat until hot. Brown the pork chops on both sides. Now add the chicken broth, onions, garlic and any other spices that you might like into the frying pan. Simmer on low heat for about an hour. The pork chops are tender and not dried out.

Easy Potato Bread

Ingredients:

2 t Yeast

3 c Bread flour

1/4 c Instant potato flakes

1/2 T Salt

1 1/2 T Butter

1 1/2 T Sugar

3/4 c Milk

3/8 c Water

Directions:

Place all ingredients in bread pan and start. Allow to cool 1 hour before slicing

Easy Sourdough Biscuits

Ingredients:

4 1/2 c Self-rising flour

2 c Buttermilk

2/3 c Cooking oil

2 pk Yeast

2 tb Sugar

1 ts Soda

Directions:

Mix all ingredients. Keep tightly covered in refrigerator. Take out as needed and knead with a little extra flour and bake.

Easy Spaghetti

Ingredients:

1 pk Angel Hair Pasta

1 cn Pasta Ready Tomatoes

1 c Diced Ham or Pepperoni

1 ts Margarine

2 c Shredded Mozarella Cheese

ds Salt and Pepper

Cook pasta, drain and add the remainder of the ingredients.

59. Easy Scrambled Egg Muffins

1 cn Spam (12 oz.)

4 6 Eggs

4 6 Slices American cheese

Directions:

Slice Spam into 4-6 square slices. Broil or heat in skillet. Scramble 4-6 eggs. Layer eggs, Spam and one slice of cheese between toasted English muffin halves. Heat 10 seconds in microwave or until cheese melts. Serves 4-6.

Easy Taco Dip

Ingredients:

1 1/2 c Mayonnaise

1 1/2 c Sour cream

1 pk (1.25 oz) taco seasoning mix

Assorted chips *OR* Fresh vegetable dippers

Directions:

Mix mayonnaise, sour cream and taco mix till blended, chill. Serve with chips or vegetables. Makes 3 cups.

Easy Taco Salad

Ingredients:

1 lb Ground beef

1 pk (1 1/4 oz) taco seasoning

1 md Head lettuce, shredded

2 md Tomatoes, seeded and chopped

1 c Bottled Catalina dressing

4 c To 5 corn chips, crushed

2 c (8 oz) shredded cheddar cheese

Directions:

Brown ground beef; drain well. Put in taco seasoning. Combine beef, lettuce, tomatoes, dressing, corn chips and cheese in a large serving bowl; toss well. Serve immediately.

Easy Tacos

Ingredients:

1 lb Lean ground beef

1 (8-oz) can tomato sauce

1 ts Mexican flavor instant bouillon

2 tb Water

1 Taco shells

Directions:

In large skillet, brown meat; pour off fat. Add sauce, bouillon and water; cook 10 minutes. Serve in taco shells; garnish as desired.

Easy Turkey Sloppy Joes

Ingredients:

1 1/2 lb Ground turkey

1/2 c Catsup

1 md Onion, diced

2 tb Dijon mustard

1/2 ts Seasoning salt

1/4 ts Garlic powder

Non stick spray

4 Large hamburger rolls or rolls of your choice, split

Directions:

Either use a non-stick skillet or spray a skillet with non-stick spray. Add ground turkey and onion, and cook until meat is no longer pink.

Add other ingredients, and simmer until thickened to your choosing.

Serve as you would sloppy joes, on split rolls.

Extra Easy Coffee Cake

Ingredients:

1/4 c Sugar

1/2 ts Cinnamon

1 cn 10oz. Hungry Jack Flaky biscuits

1/4 c Semi-sweet choc. chips

1/4 c Peanut butter chips

2 tb Margarine, melted

Directions:

Heat oven to 400 degrees. Grease 8 or 9 inch round cake pan. In 1 gallon plastic bag or large bowl, combine sugar and cinnamon; mix well. Separate dough into 10 biscuits; cut each biscuit into 4 pieces. Drop 5 pieces at a time into cinnamon mixture; toss to coat. Remove biscuits with slotted spoon; place in greased pan. Repeat with remaining pieces. Sprinkle with chips; drizzle with melted margarine. Bake fo 18 to 23 minutes or until biscuits are deep golden brown. Let stand 5 minutes; remove from pan. Serve warm.

Extra Easy Lasagna

Ingredients:

3/4 lb Ground beef

3 c Prego Traditional Spaghetti Sauce

15 oz Ricotta cheese

8 oz Shredded mozzarella cheese

6 Uncooked lasagna noodles

1/4 c Water

Directions:

In 10 inch skillet over medium high heat, cook beef until browned, stirring to separate meat. Spoon off fat. Add spaghetti sauce, heat through, stirring occasionally.

In 2 quart oblong baking dish, spread 1-1/2 cups meat mixture. Top with 3 uncooked lasagna noodles, half of the ricotta cheese and half of the mozzarella cheese. Repeat layers. Top with remaining meat mixture.

Slowly pour water around inside edges of baking dish. Cover tightly with foil. Bake at 375 degrees (f) for 45 minutes. Uncover; bake 10 minutes more. Let stand 10 minutes before serving.

Makes 8 main dish servings.

Fast And Easy Pizza

Ingredients:

1 pk English muffins

1 Pizza sauce

6 oz Mozzarella cheese

1 lb Hamburger

Directions:

Spread sauce on muffins. Top with meat and cheese. Microwave for about 1 minute.

Graham Cracker Quickie

Ingredients:

3 Eggs

1 c Sugar

1 c Chopped walnuts

1 c Graham cracker crumbs

ds Salt

Directions:

Beat eggs thoroughly and add sugar. Fold in walnuts and crumbs, also salt. Spread in a 9 inch greased pie pan. Bake for 25 minutes at 325 degrees. Serve warm with whipped cream on top. Chewy and delicious.

Greek style potato salad

Ingredients:

1 1/2 -2 lbs. potatoes washed

1/2 c Crumbled feta cheese thoroughly rinsed and drained

1 Medium onion peeled, cut in half, then thinly sliced

1/2 c Fresh parsley, coarsely chopped

1/2 ts Salt free extra spicy season

3 ts Salt free garlic & herb season

1 ts Oregano

1/3 c Lemon juice

2 tb Olive oil

2 tb Vinegar

Directions:

Boil potatoes until firm but tender. Do not overcook (15-20 minutes). Cool by placing pot of potatoes in sink and gently running cold water over potatoes. Drain thoroughly. Cut potatoes into 1/2 inch cubes. Place in a large bowl with the rest of the ingredients and toss lightly, mixing well.

Honey Butter

Ingredients:

1 c Butter

1/3 c Honey

Directions:

Whip butter in a food processor or blender and add honey slowly while continuing to mix.

Serve on rolls, muffins or bread.

Light And Easy Lasagna

Ingredients:

3 md Onions, chopped

3 Garlic cloves, finely chopped

56 oz Italian-style plum tomatoes, undrained

24 oz Italian tomato paste

1 c Chopped fresh parsley

2 ts Dried leaf oregano, crushed

1/2 ts Dried leaf thyme, crushed

1/2 ts Dried marjoram, crushed

1/2 ts Freshly ground pepper

1/2 lb Lasagna noodles

1 lb Part-skim ricotta cheese

1/2 lb Part-skim mozzarella cheese

2 oz Imported Parmesan cheese, grated

Directions: Put onions and garlic in large saucepan. Cook, covered, over low heat until tender, adding a little water if necessary to prevent scorching. Add tomatoes, tomato paste, parsley, oregano, thyme, marjoram and pepper. Simmer, covered, stirring occasionally, about 2 hours. Cook lasagna noodles in boiling water until al dente, about 12 minutes. Drain in colander; rinse with cold water. Drain well.

Heat oven to 350 degrees. Cover bottom of lightly oiled 13 by 9-inch baking dish with 1/4 of the sauce. Add layer of lasagna noodles. Top with 1/3 of the ricotta cheese, then 1/3 of the mozzarella. Sprinkle with 1/4 of the Parmesan cheese. Cover with 1/4 of the sauce. Repeat procedure 2 more times. Sprinkle remaining Parmesan cheese on top.

Bake until sauce is bubbly and cheese is melted, about 45 minutes. Let stand 10 minutes before serving.

Light And Easy Picante Fish (microwave)

Ingredients:

1 1/2 Cup fresh mushrooms

1 md Green and/or red bell pepper seeded and cut into 1 inch pieces (3/4 cup)

1 sm Onion halved and sliced

2 tb Chicken broth or water

4 Fish fillets (4-ounce each) 3/4" thick

1 c Picante sauce or salsa

2 tb Grated parmesan cheese

Directions:

In a 1 1/2 quart microwave-safe casserole combine mushrooms, pepper, onion and broth. Cook, covered, on 100% power (high) 5-6 minutes or until tender, stirring once. In an 8 x 8 x 2 inch microwave- safe baking dish place fish fillets in an even layer, tucking under thin parts. Cook, covered, on high 4-5 minutes or until fish just flakes with a fork. Drain juices. With a slotted spoon, place vegetables on top of fish; sprinkle with oregano. Spoon salsa over vegetables. Cook, uncovered, 1-2 minutes or until heated through. Sprinkle with parmesan.

Longhorn Quick Chili Dip

Ingredients:

1 c Cottage Cheese

15 oz Chili With Beans; 1 can

1 tb Hot Sauce

1 tb Lemon Juice

1 1/2 ts Cumin; Ground

3/4 c Cheddar; Sharp, Shredded

Directions:

Cream the cottage cheese in a blender or food processor or with an electric mixer. Blend the chili in, mixing well. Add the hot sauce, lemon juice and cumin. Pour into a bowl and blend in the cheddar cheese, reserving a little for a garnish. Cover and chill. Makes about 3 3/4 cups of dip.

Make-it-easy Beef Potpie

Ingredients:

1 lb Boneless beef top sirloin steak, cut 3/4 inch thick

1 tb Vegetable oil

8 oz Small mushrooms, quartered

1 md Onion, sliced

1 Garlic clove, crushed

1 Jar beef gravy

1 10 oz package frozen peas and carrots

1/4 ts Dried thyme

1 Can (8oz) refrigerated

Crescent dinner rolls

Directions:

Preheat oven to 375 degrees. Trim fat from steak. Halve steak lengthwise, then crosswise into 1/4 inch thick strips. In large ovenproof skillet, heat oil over medium-high heat until hot. Add beef in 2 batches and stir-fry 1 to 2 minutes, until outside surface is no longer pink. Do not overcook. Remove from skillet with slotted spoon; set aside. In same skillet, cook mushrooms, onion, garlic and 1/4 cup water, stirring frequently, 3 minutes, until onion is tender. Stir in gravy, vegetables and thyme. Bring to a boil; remove from heat. Stir in reserved beef. Separate crescent rolls into 8 triangles. Starting from wide ends, roll up halfway; arrange over beef mixture so pointed ends are directed toward center. Bake 17 to 19 minutes, until crescent rolls are deep golden brown. Can substitute a 9 inch square baking pan for ovenproof skillet.

Pasta Susanna

Ingredients:

Cooked pasta

Chopped vegetables (i.e. Mushrooms, Bell Peppers, Broccoli, Zucchini/Summer Squash)

Spinach

Onions

Garlic

Veggie broth

1 cn Diced tomatoes and broth

Directions:

In large non-stick skillet, saute onions & mushrooms & garlic. After a while, add spinach if frozen. Wait until spinach thaws, then add your other veggies. You may want to add some veggie broth. Before they're quite done, add 1 can (more if you like tomatoes, or if you're feeding lots (3 or more) people) of diced tomatoes with their sauce. Stir until tomatoes start to warm up, then add the cooked pasta. Stir all together. Spice as desired. (Basil, oregano, and dill is good.) Don't forget freshly ground pepper.

Quick And Chewy Chocolate Drops

Ingredients:

8 oz Hershey's semi-sweet baking chocolate, broken into pieces

1/4 c Butter or margarine; softened (1/2 stick)

1/2 c Sugar

1 Egg

1 1/2 ts Vanilla extract

1/2 c All purpose flour

1/4 ts Baking powder

1/2 c Chopped nuts; (optional)

Directions:

Heat oven to 350 deg F. In small microwave-safe bowl, place chocolate. Microwave at high (100%) 1 1/2 to 2 minutes or until chocolate is melted when stirred; cool slightly. In large mixer bowl, beat butter and sugar until well blended. Add egg and vanilla; beat well. Blend in melted chocolate, flour and baking powder. Stir in nuts, if desired. Drop by rounded teaspoonfuls onto un-greased cookie sheet. Bake 8 to 10 minutes or until almost set. Cool slightly. Remove from cookie sheet to wire rack. Cool completely. About 2 dozen cookies.

Sue McNair

Quick And Comfy Macaroni And Cheese

Ingredients:

2 c Macaroni;uncooked

2 c Mozzarella or Cheddar cheese shredded

1 1/2 c Plain yogurt or Sour cream

1 1/3 c Ham; cooked, diced, opt.

1 c Cottage cheese or ricotta

1 Egg; lightly beaten

1/4 ts -each salt & pepper

Directions:

In large pot of boiling, salted water, cook macaroni until tender but firm; drain. In large bowl, combine 1 1/2 c of the mozzarella, plain yogurt or sour cream, ham, cottage cheese, egg, salt and pepper. Add macaroni and mix well. Pour mixture into greased 8" square baking pan, sprinkle with remaining mozzarella. Bake, uncovered in 350F oven for 30 minutes or until bubbly. Broil for 2 minutes or till lightly golden.

SERVES:4

Quick And Creamy Applesauce Dessert

Ingredients:

1/2 c Applesauce; unsweetened

1/2 c Nonfat yogurt

1/2 ts Vanilla extract

1/2 ts Apple pie spice

2 ts Sugar

Directions:

Combine all ingredients in a bowl. Mix thoroughly. Serve right away or chill for later serving. This was altered to low-fat from the original recipe. Also to reduce the calories you can use a sugar substitute to equal the sugar.

Quick And Dirty Yucatan Tacos

Ingredients:

1/4 lb Lean ground beef

1 Habanero, minced

Garlic powder- approx 1/8 Teaspoon

Lime juice 2 Tablespoons

1 oz Hot sauce

Directions:

Put the meat in a skillet and add the garlic powder and cook constantly stirring the meat so it breaks up into chunks. After the outside of the meat is browned but not cooked through add the minced Habanero, lime juice and hot sauce. Cook until done. Put into a taco & enjoy.

Quick And Easy Chocolate Brownies

Ingredients:

1/2 c Sugar

1/4 c Evaporated milk

1/4 c Butter or margarine; (1/2 stick)

8 oz Hershey's semi-sweet baking chocolate, broken into pieces

2 Eggs

1 ts Vanilla extract

3/4 c All-purpose flour

1/4 ts Baking soda

1/4 ts Salt

3/4 c Chopped nuts; (optional)

Directions:

Heat oven to 350 deg F. Grease 9 inch square baking pan. In medium saucepan, combine sugar, evaporated milk and butter. Cook over medium heat, stirring constantly, until mixture boils; remove from heat. Add chocolate, stirring until melted; beat in eggs and vanilla. Stir in flour, baking soda, salt and nuts, if desired, until well blended. Pour into prepared pan. Bake 30 to 35 minutes or until brownies just begin to pull away from sides of pan. Cool completely in pan on wire rack. Cut into squares. About 16 brownies.

Quick And Easy Fudgey Brownies

Ingredients:

4 oz Hershey's Unsweetened Baking Chocolate Broken Into pieces

3/4 c Butter or Margarine

2 c Sugar

3 Eggs

1 1/2 ts Vanilla extract

1 c All-purpose flour

1 c Chopped nuts; (optional)

Directions:

Heat oven to 350 degrees Fahrenheit. Grease 13x9x2-inch baking pan. In large microwave-safe bowl, place chocolate and butter. Microwave at HIGH (100%) 1-1/2 to 2 minutes or until chocolate is melted and mixture is smooth when stirred. Add sugar; stir with spoon until well blended. Add eggs and vanilla; mix well. Add flour and nuts, if desired; stir until well blended. Spread into prepared pan. Bake 30 to 35 minutes or until wooden pick inserted in center comes out almost clean. Cool completely in pan on wire rack. Frost, if desired. Cut into squares. About 24 brownies.

Quick And Easy Lemon Cheesecake

Ingredients:

1 Graham cracker crust, baked

8 oz Pkg cream cheese

2 c Milk

1 pk Lemon instant pudding

Whipped cream, optional

Directions:

In a small mixer bowl, beat the cream cheese until creamy. Gradually add the milk; beat until well blended. Add the pudding; beat 1 minute. Pour into cooled crust. Chill well. Top with a sprinkling of graham cracker crumbs and serve with whipped cream, if desired.

Quick and Easy Mexican Bean Soup

Ingredients:

4 sl Bacon; diced

1 md Onion; chopped

30 oz Pinto beans (2 15 oz. cans); un-drained

1 cn Chicken broth

1/2 c Water

1/4 c Loosely packed cilantro; (up to 1/3)

1/3 c Picante sauce

Directions:

In a 3-quart saucepan, cook bacon until crisp. Remove with slotted spoon. Cook onion in drippings until tender but not brown. Return bacon to saucepan. Add remaining ingredients and bring to a boil, stirring occasionally. Reduce heat. Cover and simmer 15 minutes.

Quick And Easy Pumpkin Bread

Ingredients:

1 1/2 c Sugar

1 2/3 c Flour

1/4 ts Baking powder

1 ts Baking soda

3/4 ts Salt

1/2 ts Ground cloves

1/2 ts Nutmeg

1/2 ts Cinnamon

1/2 c Vegetable oil

1/2 c Water

1 c Mashed pumpkin

2 Eggs

1/2 c Nuts, optional

Directions:

Sift dry ingredients together. Stir in remaining ingredients. Pour batter into buttered and floured loaf pan. Bake 1 hour at 350.

Quick And Easy Pumpkin Pie

Ingredients:

2 Eggs, slightly beaten

1 Can sweetened cond. milk

1 Can pumpkin

1/4 ts Cloves

1/2 ts Salt

1/2 ts Ginger

1 ts Cinnamon

1/2 ts Vanilla

1 Unbaked pie shell

Directions:

Mix all ingredients in order given. Pour into unbaked shell. Bake in hot oven 425 degrees for 15 min. then reduce to 350 degrees and bake until knife inserted in middle comes out clean.

Quick And Easy Shortbread

Ingredients:

12 oz Plain flour

8 oz Butter or margarine

4 oz Caster sugar

Directions:

Mix together all the ingredients in a machine using a pastry blade. Roll out to about 1/4-inch thick and cut large round biscuits with pastry cutters.

Bake for 30 to 40 minutes at 325 degrees F

Quick And Easy Tarragon Chicken

Ingredients:

2 tb Butter or margarine

1 tb Vegetable oil

4 Chicken breasts halves skinned and boned

3/4 c Dry white wine or vermouth

2 ts Dijon mustard

1 tb Chopped fresh tarragon or 1 tsp dried

1/2 ts Salt

Freshly ground pepper

3/4 c Heavy cream

Directions:

In a large frying pan, melt butter in oil over medium-high heat. Add chicken breasts and cook, turning once, until lightly browned, about 4 minutes a side. Remove and set aside.

Add wine to the pan. Bring to a boil, scraping up brown bits from bottom of pan with a wooden spoon. Stir in mustard, tarragon, salt and pepper to taste. whisk in cream and boil until mixture thickens slightly, about 3 minutes.

Return chicken to pan; turn in sauces to coat and simmer 7-1/2 minutes until chicken is tender. remove chicken to a serving platter, spoon sauce over it.

Quick And Easy Vanilla Ice Cream

Ingredients:

3 c Milk

4 Inch piece vanilla bean or

1 2 teaspoons vanilla extract

6 Egg yolks

1 1/4 c Superfine sugar

pn Salt

Directions:

Slowly heat the milk and vanilla pod (bean), halved lengthwise. When almost boiling, remove the pan from the heat and set aside to infuse for about 20 minutes. Beat the egg yolks, sugar and salt together, until the mixture is very pale and the whisk leaves a trail. Slowly add the strained warm milk, whisking all the time. Return the mixture to the pan and cook over a very low heat, stirring constantly, until the custard is thick enough to coat the back of wooden spoon. Set the custard aside and stir it occasionally while it cools. Add the vanilla essence (extract), if using Pour into freezer trays and still freeze, whisking the mixture once or twice during freezing

Quick And Easy Waffles

Ingredients:

4 Eggs

1 c Milk

1 tb Baking powder

1/2 ts Salt (optional)

2 c Flour

1/2 c Butter; melted

1 tb Sugar

1 ts Vanilla (optional)

Directions:

Beat eggs and sugar until light and foamy. Add cooled melted butter, milk and vanilla extract. Sift flour and baking powder and add to egg mixture. Add salt & beat well. Bake and serve.

Quick And Sassy Cocktail Bites

Ingredients:

1 1.25 oz pkg chili seasoning

1/2 c Water

1/4 c Catsup

1 tb Brown sugar

1 tb Cider vinegar

1 ts Yellow mustard

1 lb Smoked sausage; sliced and halved

Directions:

Combine the first 6 sauce ingredients in a 2-quart saucepan. Bring to a boil, t urn down heat and simmer for 15 minutes. Add the cubed smoked sausage and cook on medium for another 15 minutes, stirring a few times. Serve in a chafing dish or from a small platter with toothpicks.

Quick And Simple Pasta Salad

Ingredients:

250 Grams uncooked pasta

1 Tin ratatouille

Cook pasta, rinse under cold tap until cold. Mix with ratatouille.

Easier than anyone would believe possible!

116. Quick and Simple Souffle

1 tb Oil (or non-stick spray)

3 Eggs; well beaten -OR- egg replacer

1/2 c Milk or milk substitute

1 tb Honey

1/2 ts Vanilla extract

1/2 c multi Blend Flour

2 ts Non-alum baking powder

1/4 ts Nutmeg

Directions:

Preheat oven to 450 F. Oil a 9" x 9" cake pan. Mix liquid ingredients together. Mix dry ingredients together. Combine mixtures. Pour batter into pan and bake 15 minutes. Serve while hot with honey or syrup and/or fruit. Try with fruit yogurt. Makes 2 large or 4 small servings.

Quick And Spicy Beans

Ingredients:

1 cn Garbanzo beans

1 cn Great northern whites

1 cn Pinto beans

1 cn Kidney beans

1 cn Lentils

1 pk Lipton's French Onion soup

2 Generous tablespoons Kozlowski Farms South of the Border no fat Dressing.

3 tb Hain's honey barbeque sauce

Directions:

Heat all the ingredients. Simply great!

Quick And Spicy Chicken And Rice

Ingredients:

2 c Water

1/4 ts Salt

2 c Uncooked instant rice

3 c Frozen broccoli cuts

1 8oz jar pasteurized process cheese sauce with Jalapeno peppers

8 oz Cooked chicken breast; cubed

Directions:

In large saucepan, bring water and salt to a boil. Add rice and broccoli; return to a boil. Boil 1 minute. Remove from heat; cover and let stand 5 minutes.

Stir in cheese sauce and chicken; cook over low heat for 2-4 minutes or until thoroughly heated, stirring occasionally.

Quick Apple Muffins

Ingredients:

1 Stick butter

1/2 c Light brown sugar

1 ts Cinnamon.

Directions:

In a small mixing bowl cream together:

Split 6 English muffins, toast, then spread each muffin half with 1 Tbl of the butter-sugar mixture. Mix remaining butter-sugar mixture with a 20 oz can drained, sliced pie apples and distribute over muffins. Broil 4 min to heat apples and melt butter mixture.

Quick Apple Sauce

Ingredients:

4 sm Apples peeled

1/3 c Water

Cinnamon or nutmeg to taste

Directions:

Wash and slice applies into a 2 quart glass casserole dish. Add water and cover. Cook 5-7 minutes until fruit is soft cooked but not mush. Stir in seasonings. Let rest 5 minutes before eating. Delicious warm or cold.

Quick Baked Pasta Family Style

Ingredients:

2 tb Olive oil

1 lb Ground beef, lean

2 cl Garlic; crushed

1/2 c Half and half

3/4 c Marinara sauce

3/4 lb Penne pasta

1/4 c Parmesan cheese; grated

1 ts Dried oregano

1/2 ts Dried rosemary

Salt and pepper; to taste

1 c Mozzarella cheese; grated Or swiss cheese; for topping

Directions:

Bring 4 quarts of water to a boil. Heat a large frying pan and add oil, beef and garlic. Saute until the meat is tender and then drain excess fat. Add all remaining ingredients except the Mozzarella cheese and pasta. Simmer the mixture while pasta cooks until al dente. Drain pasta and mix it with the sauce. Pour all into a 3 quart baking dish and top with the remaining cheese. Bake uncovered at 350F for 25 minutes or until bubbly hot.

Quick Barbecue Beef Bake

Ingredients:

1 lb Ground beef

3/4 c Chopped onion

18 oz Barbecue sauce

2 c Shredded cheddar cheese

2 c Bisquick Original or Reduced Fat baking mix

1 c Milk

2 Eggs

Directions:

Heat oven to 400 degrees F. Cook ground beef and 1/2 cup of the onion in 10" skillet until beef is brown; drain. Stir in barbecue sauce. Spoon into un-greased 13x9x2" baking dish; sprinkle with cheese.

Stir baking mix, milk and eggs until blended. Pour over beef mixture. Sprinkle with remaining onion.

Bake 25-27 minutes or until crust is light golden brown.

Quick Barbecue Sauce

Ingredients:

1/4 c Finely Chopped Onion

1 Clove Garlic, Finely Chopped

2 tb Butter Or Margarine

1 c Catsup

1/4 c Brown Sugar, Firmly Packed

1/4 c Lemon Juice

1 tb Worcestershire Sauce

1 ts Prepared Mustard

1/8 ts Hot Pepper Sauce

Directions:

In small saucepan, cook onion and garlic in margarine until tender. Add remaining ingredients; bring to a boil. Reduce heat; simmer uncovered 15 to 20 minutes. Use as basting sauce for pork, chicken or beef. Refrigerate leftovers. MICROWAVE: In 1-qt glass measure, microwave margarine on full power (high) 30 to 45 seconds or until melted. Add Onion and Garlic. Microwave on full power (high) 1 1/2 to 2 minutes, or until tender. Add remaining ingredients; cover with waxed paper. Microwave on full power (high) 3 to 5 minutes or until mixture boils. Microwave on 2/3rds power (medium-high) 4 to 5 mins. to blend flavors. Proceed as above.

Quick Bean and Cheese Enchiladas

Ingredients:

2 c Cooked Idaho Pinto beans OR Pink or Small Red Beans

1/2 c Bottled salsa -OR- picante sauce

8 Corn tortillas

1/2 lb Cheddar cheese, divided

20 oz Enchilada sauce

Shredded lettuce

Sour cream

Directions:

Mash beans with salsa. Spoon beans down center of each tortilla, dividing evenly Cut half of cheese into 8 sticks. Place 1 stick over beans on each tortilla. Roll tortilla to enclose cheese and beans. Place, seam-side down, in greased shallow baking dish. Pour enchilada sauce over all. Grate remaining cheese and sprinkle over sauce. Bake in preheated 350-degree F oven for 15 to 18 minutes. Garnish with lettuce and sour cream. Makes 8 enchiladas.

Quick Beef And Cheese Burritos

Ingredients:

1 lb Lean ground beef

1 1/4 c Chunky salsa

8 oz Monterey jack cheese, cubed

8 Flour tortillas, warmed

Sliced lettuce

Chopped tomato

Sliced black olives

Directions:

Brown the beef in a skillet over medium-high heat until no longer pink. Pour off drippings. Stir in salsa and cheese; heat until cheese melts.

To serve, divide filling among tortillas. Fold bottom edge of each tortilla up over filling; fold sides to center, overlapping edges. Top with lettuce, tomato and olives.

Sue McNair

Quick Beef Casserole

Ingredients:

1 lb Ground beef

1 md Onion, finely chopped

1 cn Spanish rice (15-oz)

1 cn Stewed tomatoes (16-oz)

1/2 c Cheddar cheese - 1/4" cubes

Directions:

Fry beef and onions until browned. Drain. Add rice, tomatoes, and cheese. Simmer until mixture is heat through and cheese is melted. Serve with salad and toasted garlic bread.

Quick Beef Minestrone

Ingredients:

1/2 lb Ground beef

16 oz Frozen Italian mixed vegetables

2 cn Water

2 c Shredded cabbage

Grated Parmesan cheese

1 cn Condensed tomato soup

1 ts Dried basil

1/2 c Uncooked elbow macaroni

Directions:

In a soup pot, cook beef until well browned. Drain off fat. Stir in frozen vegetables, undiluted soup, water and basil. Heat to boiling, stirring occasionally. Simmer 15 minutes. Stir in cabbage and elbow macaroni. Cook until tender. Sprinkle with grated cheese. SERVES 6.

Quick Beef Pie

Ingredients:

1 1/2 lb Ground beef

1 md Onion, chopped

1/2 ts Salt

1 cn Condensed tomato soup 10 1/2 oz. size

1 cn Cut green beans, drained 16 oz.

1/4 ts Pepper

2 c Potatoes, seasoned & mashed

1/2 c Chedder cheese, shredded

Directions:

Crumble beef into large fry pan. Add onion and salt, and cook until browned. Drain off excess fat. Add soup, green beans and pepper. Simmer for 5 minutes. Pour into a greased 2 quart casserole. Spread mashed potatoes over the top. Sprinkle with cheese. Bake at 350 degrees for 20 minutes.

Quick Beef Sausage

Ingredients:

4 lb Lean Ground Beef

1/4 c Morton Tender Quick Salt

2 ts Pepper

2 ts Liquid Smoke

1 ts Garlic Powder

Directions:

In a large bowl combine ground beef and quick salt. Mix and leave overnight in the refrigerator. Next day add pepper, liquid smoke and garlic powder. Mix well, divide into 3 rolls. Bake at 225 degrees F for 4 hours on broiler pan on lower rack in oven. Wrap in paper towels to absorb grease. Refrigerate or freeze.

Quick Beef Stew

Ingredients:

2 tb Vegetable oil

1 md Onion, finely chopped

1 Bay leaf

8 oz Can sliced carrots, drained

16 oz Can tiny white potatoes, drained

1/2 ts Salt

1/8 ts Pepper

1/4 ts Celery salt

2 c Beef gravy (recipe)

2 c To 3 c cubed cooked beef

8 oz Can green peas, drained

Directions:

In a deep, 2-quart, heat-resistant, non-metallic casserole, heat oil in Microwave Oven 2 minutes. Add onion and heat, uncovered, in Microwave Oven 3 minutes or until tender. Stir occasionally. Add bay leaf, carrots, potatoes, salt, pepper, celery salt, beef gravy and beef; stir to combine. Heat, covered, in Microwave Oven 6 to 7 minutes or until almost heated. Taste and correct seasoning, if necessary, with additional salt and pepper. Remove bay leaf and discard. Add peas and heat, covered, in Microwave Oven 2 to 3 minutes or until heated through.

Quick Biscuit Mix

Ingredients:

2 3/4 c Wheat flour

1/2 c Soy flour; 2 T

1 1/4 ts -salt

1/2 c Inst dry milk;less 1 T

2 1/2 tb Baking powder

1 c Wheat germ

Directions:

Combine all ingredients store in sealed container.

Makes 5 c

Quick Biscuits

Ingredients:

2 c Flour

5 ts Baking powder

1 ts Salt

1/4 c Shortening

1 c Milk

Directions:

Mix and sift the dry ingredients; rub in the shortening and mix with the milk to a soft, thick dough. Drop by spoonfuls onto a well-greased tin and bake in a quick oven (425) for about 15 minutes. These are best when made with butter and come out of the oven as thin, crusty biscuits rather than the thicker variety.

Twelve biscuits.

Quick Blueberry Muffins

Ingredients:

1 c Vanilla ice cream, softened

1 c Self-rising flour

1 c Fresh blueberries

1 tb Butter or margarine, melted

2 tb Sugar

Directions:

In a medium bowl, mix ice cream and flour. Fold in blueberries. Spoon into six greased muffin cups. Bake at 375 for 20-25 minutes or until muffins test done. While hot, brush muffin tops with butter and sprinkle with sugar. Serve warm.

Quick Bread Sticks

Ingredients:

10 Low-fat refrigerated biscuit dough

1 1/4 c Rice cereal, coarsely crushed

1/2 ts Salt

3 tb Skim milk

1 1/2 tb Grated Parmesan Cheese

Directions:

Cut each biscuit into thirds. Roll each piece into a 4 inch stick. Combine cereal and salt. Roll each stick in milk and then in cereal. Place on baking sheet and sprinkle with cheese. Bake at 400 degrees for 8-10 minutes or until golden brown.

Quick Broccoli And Rice Casserole

Ingredients:

10 oz Pk Frozen Broccoli With Cheese Sauce

1/2 c Quick Cooking Rice

1/2 c Whole Milk

1 c Cooked Chicken, Ham Or Turkey -- Cubed

2 tb Parmesan -- Grated

Directions:

Follow package directions for frozen Broccoli w/Cheese Sauce.

Turn into a (1 Qt.) casserole. Add the chicken, ham or turkey. Add the rice, milk and cheese. Blend thoroughly. Cover. Microwave on high until the rice is tender (about 6 minutes), stirring once. Serve

Quick Brown Betty

Ingredients:

3 c Tart apples

1 1/2 c Coarse bread crumbs

1/4 c Butter, melted

1 c Brown sugar

1/2 ts Cinnamon OR nutmeg

1/2 c Water

Directions:

Preheat oven to 325 degrees. Mix first four ingredients together in a 10 x 6 x 2 inch baking dish. Sprinkle with the cinnamon. Pour water over the top.

Bake 45 to 50 minutes.

Quick Cake Doughnuts

Ingredients:

1/4 c Butter or margarine; softened

1 c Sugar

1 ea Egg

1 t Baking soda

1 c Buttermilk

4 c All-purpose flour

1 t Baking powder

Vegetable oil

2 c Sifted sugar

2 tb Milk

Directions:

Cream butter; gradually add sugar, beating well. Add egg; beat well. Dissolve soda in buttermilk. Combine flour and baking powder; add to creamed mixture alternately with buttermilk mixture, beginning and ending with the flour mixture. Divide the dough in half. Working with one portion at a time, place dough on a floured surface; roll out to 1/4-inch thickness. Cut dough with a floured doughnut cutter. Heat 3 to 4 inches of oil to 375 degrees F; drop in 3 or 4 doughnuts at a time. Cook about 1 minute or until golden brown on one side; turn and cook other side about 1 minute. Drain on paper towels. Combine powdered sugar and milk, beating well; drizzle over warm doughnuts.

Note: Doughnuts may be sprinkled with a cinnamon-sugar mixture or powdered sugar instead of the powdered-sugar glaze.

Quick California Pizza

Ingredients:

1 cn Stewed tomatoes (14.5 oz)

1 Bread shell,large

1 tb Olive oil

1 cn Mushrooms,sliced (3 oz)

1 tb Parsley

1/3 c Romano cheese,grated

Directions:

Drain tomatoes and save juice. Add olive oil to reserved tomato juice and brush over the top of bread shell. Arrange tomatoes and mushrooms on top. Sprinkle with parsley and Romano cheese. Bake 10 minutes at 450 degrees F.

Quick Candied Yams

Ingredients:

1 cn Yams (large can)

1 Caramel topping (jar)

1/4 lb Butter

Marshmallows

Directions:

Put drained yams into a baking dish. Pour caramel topping over the yams. Add the butter in slices over the top of the caramel topping. Bake at 350 degrees until hot and bubbly. Add marshmallows and bake until the marshmallows are brown and melted.

Quick Cape Breton Chowder

Ingredients:

1 lb Cod fillets; frozen *

1 tb Butter

1/2 c Onion; finely chopped

10 oz Cream of celery soup

14 oz Clam chowder

1 c Milk

1/2 c Water

Parsley; chopped

Directions:

Partially thaw fish. Cut in 1 inch (2 cm) pieces. Saute onion in butter until translucent. Stir in soups, milk and water. Slowly bring to a boil. Add fish and simmer 5 to 8 minutes or until flesh is opaque and flakes easily. Sprinkle with parsley.

* or Boston bluefish, haddock, turbot

Quick Caramel Rolls

Ingredients:

1 Loaf frozen bread dough

3/4 c Nuts

1/2 pk Butterscotch pudding (no instant)

1/2 c Brown sugar

1/2 c Margarine

1 ts Water

Directions:

Thaw bread for 45 minutes. Grease Bundt (or other tube pan) well with butter(margarine) and sprinkle nuts all around bottom and sides. Cut bread into 12 equal pieces and put in bottom of pan. Combine last 4 ingredients in small saucepan and cook over medium heat until bubbles form(stirring constantly) and boil one minute. Spoon over bread dough to coat each piece. Cover lightly with kitchen towel and leave on counter overnight.

In the morning, bake at 350 degrees for 15-20 minutes. Let cool for 5 minutes. Then flip onto a plate and let sauce drizzle over.

Quick Casserole

Ingredients:

1 tb Butter

1 tb Chopped onion

1 c Chopped celery

3/4 c Uncle ben's rice

1 cn Mushroom soup

1 cn Chicken & rice soup

1 cn Beef consomme

Directions:

Saute onion & celery, add to other ingredients in casserole & bake at 350 until rice is cooked approximately 1 hour.

Quick Celery-cheese Loaf

Ingredients:

3 c Flour -- sifted

1/4 c Sugar

4 ts Baking powder

1 ts Salt

1/2 c Shortening

1 c Cheddar cheese -- shredded

1/4 ts Celery seed

1 1/4 c Milk

1 Eggs

Directions:

Into large bowl, sift together flour, sugar, baking powder and salt. With pastry blender, cut in shortening until coarse crumbs form. Stir in cheese and celery seed; set aside. In small bowl, mix milk and eggs until well blended. Add milk mixture to dry ingredients; stir just until moistened. Pour batter into greased and waxed paper-lined 9x5x3 loaf pan. Bake in 350 degree oven 50 to 60 minutes, or until loaf is golden brown and toothpick inserted in center comes out clean. Cool in pan 10 minutes. Remove; peel off waxed paper. Cool on rack. Makes 1 loaf.

Quick Cheddar Bread

Ingredients:

3 3/4 c Unbleached flour

5 ts Baking powder

1/2 ts Salt

1/3 c Butter

2 1/2 c Cheddar; sharp

1 1/2 c Milk

2 ea Eggs; lg, slightly beaten

Directions:

Combine the dry ingredients, then cut the butter into the flour until the mixture resembles coarse crumbs, then add the cheddar cheese. Combine the milk and eggs then add the mixture to the cheddar mixture. Stir until just moistened, then spoon into a greased 9 X 5-inch loaf pan. Bake at 375 degrees F. hour. Remove from the pan immediately and let cool on a wire rack.

Quick Cherry Dessert

Ingredients:

1 c Butter or margarine

1 1/2 c Granulated sugar

4 Eggs

1 ts Almond extract

2 c All-purpose flour

2 ts Baking powder

1 cn (21oz) Cherry pie filling

Directions:

Powdered sugar to dust over top, optional

In a large mixing bowl, cream together the butter and sugar. Add the almond extract. Stir in the flour and baking powder. Mix until smooth. Butter a 13x9-inch cake pan. Turn the mixture into the pan. Spoon the pie filling into the cake, in 16 spots, spacing 4 spoonfuls evenly in each direction. Bake at 350 degrees F for 45 to 50 minutes or until golden and cake tests done. Filling will sink into the cake while baking. To serve, cut into 16 pieces. Place bottom side up on serving plate. Dust with powdered sugar, if used. Spoon slightly sweetened whipped cream over each serving, if desired. This is great served warm!

Note: For blueberry dessert, substitute blueberry pie filling for the cherry filling.

Quick Chicken And Biscuits

Ingredients:

3 lb Boneless chicken breast

1 pk Big Country Biscuits

1 cn Cream of chicken soup

Directions:

Place chicken in un-greased casserole. Pour soup over top. Cover. Bake at 350 for 1 hour. Put biscuits on top of chicken. Bake, uncovered, until biscuits are brown.

Quick Chicken And Noodles

Ingredients:

4 Skinless boneless chicken breast halves

1/4 ts Garlic powder

1/8 ts Paprika

1 cn (14.5 oz.) Swanson chicken broth

1/2 ts Dried basil leaves, crushed

1/8 ts Pepper

2 c Frozen broccoli, cauliflower, carrots

2 c Dry wide egg noodles

Directions:

In a medium nonstick skillet over medium-high heat, cook chicken 10 minutes or until browned. Sprinkle with garlic powder and paprika. Set chicken aside. Add broth, basil, pepper and vegetables. Heat to a boil. Stir in noodles. Return chicken to pan. Reduce heat to low. Cover and cook 10 minutes or until chicken is no longer pink. If desired, garnish with fresh basil.

Serves 4

Quick Chicken Cacciatore

Ingredients:

4 Chicken breast halves; boned skinless (1 lb total)

7 1/2 oz (1) can tomatoes; cut up

3/4 c Mushrooms; sliced fresh

1/4 c Onion; chopped

1/4 c Green pepper; chopped

3 tb Dry red wine

1 cl Garlic; minced

1 ts Oregano; crushed dried

1/4 ts Salt

1 tb Cold water

2 ts Cornstarch;

Directions:

Rinse chicken; pat dry. In a medium skillet combine undrained tomatoes, mushrooms, onion, green pepper, wine, garlic, oregano, salt, and pepper; place chicken atop vegetable mixture. Bring to boiling, reduce heat. Cover; simmer about 20 minutes or till chicken is tender and no long pink. Transfer chicken to a serving platter; keep warm. Stir together water and cornstarch; stir into skillet mixture. Cook and stir till good and bubbly. Cook and stir for 2 minutes more. Spoon sauce over chicken.

Quick Chicken Divan

Ingredients:

2 Whole chicken breasts

1 10 oz. pkg frozen broccoli spears

1 cn Cream of chicken soup; undiluted

1/2 c Hellman's(c) mayonnaise

1 tb Lemon juice

1 ds Curry powder

1/2 c Cheddar cheese; shredded

Bread crumbs;

Pepperidge farm stuffing mix

Directions:

Simmer the chicken breasts in salted water until tender, about 45 minutes. Let cool in broth. Remove meat from bones. In shallow casserole, place frozen broccoli, separated, with chicken on top. Mix together the soup, mayonnaise, lemon juice, curry, and cheese. Pour the mixture over the chicken and broccoli. Top with bread crumbs and bake at 350 degrees uncovered for 45 minutes.

Serves 4

Quick Chicken Marinara

Ingredients:

4 Chicken breasts, skinned

16 oz Marinara sauce

8 oz Mozzarella cheese, sliced thinly

Directions:

Place chicken breasts in baking pan. Cover each breast with a few slices of cheese. Pour sauce over chicken and cheese. Cover lightly with foil. Bake in 350 degree F. oven for about 40 minutes.

Spoon sauce from bottom of baking pan over chicken every 10 or 15 minutes. Remove foil for last 10 or 15 minutes of baking.

Quick Chicken Piccata

Ingredients:

4 Boneless chicken breast halves, skinned

Salt and freshly ground pepper

2 tb Butter

1 ts Vegetable oil

1/2 c Chicken broth

1/4 c Vermouth

2 tb Fresh lemon juice

1 tb Capers, drained, rinsed

Lemon slices

Directions:

Pat chicken dry. Season with salt and pepper. Melt butter with oil in heavy large skillet over medium-high heat. Add chicken and cook until springy to touch, 4 minutes per side. Remove from skillet; keep warm.

Increase heat to high. Stir broth and vermouth into skillet. Boil until reduced by half, scraping up any browned bits. Remove from heat. Mix in lemon juice and capers. Place chicken on plates and pour sauce over. Garnish chicken with lemon slices.

4 servings.

Quick Chicken Piroshki

Ingredients:

2 tb Margarine

1/4 c Chopped shallots

1 md Garlic clove, minced

2 Chopped cooked chicken breasts

1 c Cooked rice

2 tb Chopped parsley

1/8 ts Dried thyme

Salt

5-pepper blend

2 cn Crescent rolls

1 Egg, beaten

Directions:

Preheat oven to 350. In a large frying pan. melt margarine over medium heat. Add shallots and garlic and cook until tender, but not brown, about 2 minutes. Stir in chicken, rice, parsley, thyme, and salt and pepper to taste.

Separate crescent rolls into 8 squares; seal line in each square. Divide chicken mixture evenly among squares; fold to make a triangle and seal edges. Prick tops of pastry with fork, and brush with egg. Bake on an un-greased baking sheet 15 minutes until golden brown. Remove to a serving platter and keep warm until ready to serve

Quick Chili Casserole

Ingredients:

9 oz Pkg. corn chips

1 cn Chili with beans

2 c Grated cheddar cheese

2 c Chopped onions, sautéed

Directions:

Place 1/2 of corn chips in buttered casserole dish. Cover with one cup of cheese, 1 cup onion and 1/2 can of chili. Repeat except saving rest of cheese for top layer. Cook in 400 degree oven until top of cheese is melted.

Quick Clam Chowder

Ingredients:

2 ea Potato; pared and diced

1 c Leek; washed and sliced or

1/2 c Celery; sliced

1/2 c Carrot; sliced

2 ts Margarine; diet

2 c Tomato; low sodium - canned

1/4 ts Thyme

1 ea Littleneck clams; rinsed

Directions:

In 4 qt microwave casserole, combine potato, leeks or onions, celery, carrot, and margarine;cover with plastic wrap and zap on high for 6 min, until potato is softened. Add tomatoes with liquid and thyme, recover with plastic wrap and zap again on high for 5 min until potato is soft and mixture is thoroughly heated. Arrange clams hinge side out and cover again...Zap 3 min turn... Zap 3 min.Let stand 5 min and serve.

Quick Cobbler Pie

Ingredients:

1 c Flour

1 c Sugar

2 ts Baking powder

1/4 ts Salt

3/4 c Milk

Directions:

Preheat oven to 375 Mix above ingredients. Put 1/2 c. oleo in 8 x 12 baking dish and melt. Pour above mixture into oleo in baking dish. Add 1 medium sized can of sweetened fruit or 3 to 4 cups of fresh fruit. If fruit is not sweetened, add 1/2 c. sugar on top before baking. Bake about 45 min

Quick Cookies

Ingredients:

1/2 c Brown sugar

1/2 c White sugar

1/4 c Butter

1 Egg, unbeaten

1 c Flour

1 ts Baking powder

1 ts Cinnamon

1 ts Vanilla

1/3 c Chopped nuts (optional)

Directions:

Cream sugars and butter together. Mix in egg. Add flour sifted with baking powder. Add vanilla and nuts. Drop from a spoon on a lightly greased cookie sheet. Bake at 350 deg for 7 minutes. Check for cookie to be just browned on the bottom for chewy cookies.

Quick Custard Rice Pudding

Ingredients

2 c Cooked long-grain rice

2 1/2 c Milk

1 c Sugar

2 ts Vanilla

2 ts Grated lemon zest

1/4 ts Salt

6 Eggs

1/4 ts Nutmeg

Light cream or lightly sweetened whipped cream (optional)

Directions:

In a large bowl, combine the rice, 1 1/2 cups of the milk, the sugar, vanilla, lemon zest, and salt. In a small bowl, beat the remaining 1 cup milk and the eggs until thoroughly blended; stir into the rice mixture.

Pour into a 2 or 3 quart casserole. Bake in a preheated 350F oven for 30 minutes. Stir gently and dust with the nutmeg. Continue to bake 40 more minutes, or until set and lightly browned. Cool slightly, then serve warm, with cream, if desired.

Quick Dessert

Ingredients:

1 pk Raspberry Jello

1 md Jar applesauce

Graham crackers

Cool whip

Directions:

Layer pan with graham crackers. Mix together Jello and applesauce. Put on top of graham crackers. Spread Cool Whip over the top. Chill 2 hours before serving.

Quick Egg And Potato Scramble

Ingredients:

1 Fresh Idaho potato, pared and diced

1/2 c Chopped onion

1/2 c Chopped green or red pepper

6 Eggs

1/3 c Milk

1/2 ts Salt

1/8 ts Pepper

Dash garlic powder

Directions:

In 9 inch microwave-safe pie plate combine potato, onion and green pepper. Cover loosely with plastic wrap; cook on High 7 to 9 minutes or until potatoes are tender. Mix together remaining ingredients. Pour over potatoes. Loosely cover with waxed paper; cook on High 4 to 6 minutes or until eggs are just set as desired, stirring twice. Let stand 2 minutes. Makes 4 servings.

Quick Lemon-beef Stir Fry

Ingredients:

1/2 c Beef flank steak, thinly sliced

2 tb Hoisin sauce

2 ts Cornstarch

2 tb Lemon juice, fresh

1 x White pepper

1/4 c Carrots, shredded

1/4 c Mushrooms, fresh, sliced

1 ts Soy sauce

1/2 ts Sugar

1/8 ts Red chili flakes

1 ts Lemon zest, finely minced

1 x Salt

1 cn Water chestnuts, sm, sliced

1/2 c Snow peas

Directions:

Heat a wok or skillet. Add 1T vegetable oil. Add thinly sliced beef and sautee until half cooked. Combine soy, hoisin, garlic, sugar, chili, lemon and cornstarch into sauce and add to beef. When glazey, about 1 minute, add salt & white pepper to taste and stir in vegetables. Stir-fry until mushrooms and snow peas are cooked but still crunchy. Serve immediately with plain rice.

Quick Low-fat Burritos

Ingredients:

1 Tortilla

1/4 c Beans; canned

1/4 c Rice; cooked

Cilantro pesto or salsa

Lettuce; shredded

Monterey Jack; or other cheese- reduced fat variety

Directions:

Top tortilla with beans and rice; warm in the microwave. Top with cilantro pesto or salsa, shredded lettuce and a little grated low-fat cheese. Roll up and serve.

Quick Macadamia Chicken

Ingredients:

1 Garlic clove, pressed

4 Chicken breasts, boned

1/4 ts Dill

1/2 Sweet red pepper

1/4 lb Green beans (optional)

1 lg Tomato

1/8 lb Macadamia nuts

4 tb Honey

1/8 ts Sesame seeds

Sesame oil

Directions:

Slice or chop all ingredients. Saute the garlic in the sesame oil, until just fragrant. Add the dill and the chicken, and saute for about five minutes. Add the green beans and the red pepper; saute for another couple of minutes. Add the tomato and the macadamia nuts; saute another minute or two. Add the honey and the sesame seeds. Continue cooking just long enough to warm the honey.

Quick Marinated Chicken

Ingredients:

1 ea Chicken, cut-up

Marinade:

1/2 c Vinegar

1 c Vegetable oil

1 tb Ground black pepper

1 tb Salt

3 tb Worchestire sauce

2 tb Lemon juice

2 tb Thyme

1 tb Garlic salt

2 tb Mayonnaise

Directions:

Rinse chicken pieces, pat dry and place in a large plastic bag. Place marinade ingredients in a jar, cover and shake well (yes, it is ugly!) Pour marinade over chicken, squeeze out air and seal bag. Rotate several times to coat chicken. Marinade in refrigerator 1 hour to overnight. Remove chicken, saving excess marinade. Grill over hot coals or 6-7 inches from oven broiler until done (30-45 min.) , basting several times with reserved marinade.

Quick Mint Brownies

Ingredients:

20 1/2 oz Box Brownie mix

2/3 c Chocolate chips or chopped walnuts

Icing:

1/2 c Butter, room temperature

1/4 ts Salt

1 ts Peppermint extract

1 c Confectioners sugar

10 1/2 oz Chocolate fudge topping

Directions:

Prepare brownies as directed on package, stirring chocolate chips or walnut pieces into batter before baking. Let brownies cool, cut into 1 1/2-inch squares and refrigerate for 2 hours.

To prepare icing, cream together butter, salt, peppermint extract and confectioners sugar until smooth. Spread over brownies. Let icing set.

Spread chocolate fudge topping over the top of each frosted brownie square. Place the brownies in the freezer for 5-10 minutes. Remove and serve or keep in a cool spot until serving.

Quick Onion Cheese Bread

Ingredients:

3 c Flour

1 tb Baking powder

3 tb Sugar

1 c Cheddar, stale; grated

4 Scallion; chopped

1 1/2 c Beer

1 Egg; beaten

1 ts Sesame seeds

Directions:

Preheat oven to 350 degrees F. Combine flour, baking powder, sugar, cheese, and scallions. Stir beer in gently to form a thick, sticky batter. Pour batter into greased loaf pan, 8-1/2 x 4-1/2 inches. Brush top of loaf with beaten egg and sprinkle with sesame seeds. Bake in oven for 1-1/4 hours or until loaf browns. Remove from oven and cool on a wire rack.

Quick Oriental Chicken And Cashews

Ingredients:

1 1/2 Microwave spirals uncooked

1 cn (14-oz) chicken chow mein

1 c Ready to serve chicken broth

1/2 c Cashews

Soy sauce

Directions:

In 2 quart microwave safe casserole, stir together pasta, chow mein and broth. Cover; microwave at high 8-10 minutes, stirring once, or until pasta is tender. Stir in cashews and soy sauce to taste.

Quick Peanut Butter Pound Cake

Ingredients:

1 pk Yellow cake mix

3 Eggs

2/3 c Milk

1 1/2 c Creamy peanut butter

1 sm Instant vanilla pudding

Directions:

Combine all ingredients in a large mixing bowl. Blend well. Beat on medium speed for 5 minutes. Pour mixture into a greased and floured 13x9" pan. Bake at 350 degrees for 1 hour. Cool in pan 10 minutes. Remove from pan and cool completely.

Quick Pear Crumble

Ingredients:

32 oz Pear halves in juice

1/4 c Quick-cooking oats

2 tb Chopped walnuts

2 tb Golden raisins

1 tb Butter or margarine,melted

1 tb Brown sugar

1/8 ts Ground cinnamon

1/8 ts Ground ginger

Directions:

Place 8 pear halves, cut-side up, in broiler-proof pan. Combine remaining ingredients. Crumble over pears.

Broil 6" from heat 3 minutes, until browned.

Quick Pizza Sticks

Ingredients:

1 cn Ready pizza crust

1 tb Margarine or butter; melted

1/2 c Provolone cheese; shredded

1 tb Grated Romano cheese

1 ts Dried basil leaves

1/4 ts Garlic powder

1/4 ts Cayenne pepper

Directions:

Heat oven to 425 degrees F. Lightly grease large cookie sheet. Remove dough from can; unroll onto greased cookie sheet, forming 12x9" rectangle. Brush dough with margarine. In small bowl, combine provolone and romano, basil, garlic powder and ground red pepper; mix well. Sprinkle evenly over dough. With pizza cutter or knife, cut dough crosswise into 12, 1" wide strips. Cut rectangle in half lengthwise, forming 24 strips. Do not separate. Bake for 10-13 minutes or until golden brown. To separate, re-cut along perforations. Serve immediately. If desired, serve with warm pizza sauce.

Quick Pork Lo Mein

Ingredients:

8 Ozs. leftover pork roast

1 c Chopped onion

1 c Thinly sliced carrots

1 ts Minced fresh garlic

2 To 3 packages oriental-flavored noodle-soup mix with seasoning packets

1 1/2 c Water

1 c Frozen peas

6 c Coarsely shredded romaine lettuce

Directions:

Put pork, onion, carrots and garlic into a skillet and cook over medium heat for 5 to 6 minutes. Break noodles into the skillet. Stir in seasoning packets, water and pea. Bring to a boil and cook 3 to 5 minutes. Stir in lettuce and cook uncovered, stirring almost constantly, until lettuce is wilted. Serve immediately. Serves 4

Quick Potato Casserole

Ingredients:

1 lb Hash brown potatoes; frozen

1/2 ts Onion powder

1 c Sour cream

1 c Cream of mushroom soup

1 c Cheddar cheese; shredded

Parmesan cheese

Directions:

Mix all ingredients together except Parmesan. Put into greased 9x13 casserole dish. Sprinkle Parmesan over top...probably about 1/4 cup or so. Bake for 1 hour at 400 degrees F. This can be doubled easily. Also can be prepared in advance and baked just before serving.

Quick Potato Salad For One

Ingredients:

1/4 c Mayonnaise

1 tb Drained chopped roasted red pepper or pimiento, drained (optional)

1 tb Finely chopped onion

1 1/2 ts Cider vinegar

1 ts Dijon-style mustard

1/4 ts Salt

Dash pepper

1 Fresh Idaho potato, baked, cubed

Directions:

In small bowl combine first seven ingredients; mix well. Add potatoes; toss to coat well. Cover; refrigerate. Makes 1 serving.

Quick Potatoes Au Gratin

Ingredients:

16 oz Frozen Souther-style hash brown potatoes

8 oz Kraft Natural Shredded Sharp Cheddar cheese

1 cn Cream of chicken soup

1 c Miracle Whip Salad Dressing

1/2 c Chopped onion

1/8 ts Pepper

2 c Crushed Post Toasties Corn Flakes

2 tb Parkay margarine, melted

Directions:

Heat oven to 350. Mix potatoes, cheese, soup, salad dressing, onion and pepper. Spoon into 12 x 8-inch baking dish. Sprinkle with combined crushed corn flakes and margarine. Bake 45 to 55 minutes or until thoroughly heated. Makes 6 servings.

Sue McNair

Quick Pound Cake

Ingredients:

3 Eggs

1/2 c Milk

1/2 ts Vanilla extract

3 c Basic Cake Mix

Directions:

Preheat oven to 300 degrees.

Beat eggs until foamy; add milk and vanilla and continue beating.

Add dry mixture to eggs, 1/2 cup at a time, beating well after each addition.

Pour into a greased 9-inch loaf pan and bake for 1-1/2 hours.

Idea: For a fruit shortcake, pour batter into a greased 9-inch square pan and bake for 1 hour and 15 minutes. When cook, cut cake into 2-inch squares. Slice each square in half, fill with berries and juice, and replace top half. Cover with sweetened whipped cream.

Quick Quesadillas

Ingredients:

1 (7-in) Soft tortilla

1/2 ts Dijon

1/3 c Grated old cheddar

1 tb Each sliced green onions and chopped coriander or parsley

Directions:

Spread tortilla with Dijon. Sprinkle with cheddar, green onions and coriander or parsley. Roll snugly. Cover with plastic wrap. Microwave for 20 to 25 seconds. Or wrap in foil and bake at 350F for 12 minutes. Slice into 1-in. pieces and serve warm with salsa. Each tortilla makes 6 pieces.

Quick Raisin Bread

Ingredients:

2 c Flour

2 ts Baking powder

1/4 ts Baking soda

3/4 ts Salt

1/3 c Sugar

1 c Raisins

2 c Cereal flakes

1 ea Egg

1 1/2 c Buttermilk

4 tb Shortening; melted

Directions:

Dredge raisins in small amount of flour, sift dry ingredients together and add raisins and cereal. Beat eggs slightly, add milk and melted shortening, blend well with first mixture but do not overmix. Bake in greased loaf pan 350 F. about 1 hour.

Quick Rhubarb Crisp

Ingredients:

3 c Rhubarb; cut bite-size

1/3 c Sugar

2/3 c Quick oatmeal

1/3 c Flour

3/4 c Brown sugar; packed

1/2 ts Nutmeg

1/2 ts Cinnamon

1/4 c Margarine

Directions:

Place rhubarb in greased oblong microwave-safe baking dish. Combine sugar, oatmeal, flour, brown sugar and spices. Mix margarine in until crumbly, and sprinkle over rhubarb. MICROWAVE for 12 to 16 minutes on HIGH or until rhubarb is tender. About 6 servings.

258. Quick Rolls

4 c Self rising flour

2 c Buttermilk

3/4 c Oil

2 tb Sugar

4 tb Warm water

1 pk Yeast

Quick Sally Lunn

Ingredients:

4 c Cake flour; sifted

2 ts Baking powder

1/2 ts Salt

1/2 c Shortening

4 tb Sugar

1 ea Egg; beaten

1 c Milk

Directions:

Sift flour once, measure, add baking powder, salt, and sift again. Cream shortening, add sugar, cream together thoroughly. Combine egg and milk. Add flour to creamed butter and sugar, alternately with milk mixture, small amount at a time, beating after each addition until smooth. Bake in greased muffin pans, or baking sheet, in hot oven 425 F. 25 minutes, or until done.

Quick Sesame Ginger Chicken

Ingredients:

1 1/2 tb Sesame seeds, toasted

1 tb Grated fresh gingerroot

3 tb Low sodium soy sauce

3 tb Honey

6 4 oz. skinned, boned chicken

Veg. cooking oil

Directions:

Combine first 4 ingredients.

Place chicken between 2 sheets of heavy duty plastic wrap and flatten to 1/4" thickness, using meat mallet or rolling pin. Brush half of soy sauce mixture over chicken, coating both sides.

Coat grill rack with cooking spray, place on grill over med-hot coals. Place chicken on rack, grill, covered, 8 to 10 minutes or until chicken is done, turning and basting frequently with remaining soy sauce mixture

Quick Shrimp Gumbo

Ingredients:

2 tb Cooking oil

1 c Okra

1 cn Chicken gumbo

2 cn Shrimp (4 1/2 oz.)

2 tb Flour

1 cn Chicken & rice soup

1 Salt & pepper to taste

Directions:

Make roux with cooking oil and flour. Brown until dark brown color. Add okra, salt and pepper. Add soup and carefully rinsed shrimp. Simmer until hot. Serve over rice. If more vegetables are desired, add chopped bell pepper, minced garlic and green onion blades.

Quick Shrimp In Garlic Butter

Ingredients:

1/4 c Margarine

1/2 ts Garlic powder

2 ts Dried parsley flakes

1/4 ts Paprika

1 ds Ground black pepper

1 lb Small shrimp

1 ts Lemon juice

Directions:

Place margaine in custard cup or 1 cup glass measure. Add garlic powder, parsley flakes, paprika, and pepper. Microwave on High about 1 minute, or until melted. Peel and devein shrimp; spread in 10 inch round glass baking dish. Pour butter mixture evenly over shrimp. Cover with plastic wrap, making a 1" slit in plastic to vent. Microwave on High 6 to 9 minutes, stirring every 2 minutes, until shrimp are just pink and opaque. Let stand, covered, 1 minute. Sprinkle with lemon juice and garnish with fresh parsley sprigs.

Quick Southwestern Pizza

Ingredients:

1 1/2 c Bisquick Original baking mix

1/3 c Very hot water

2 c Cut-up cooked chicken

1/2 c Salsa or picante sauce

2 c Shredded mozzarella cheese (8 oz)

1/4 c Chopped onion

1/2 Bell pepper, cut into thin rings

Directions:

Move oven rack to lowest position. Heat oven to 450'F. Greast cookie sheet or 12" pizza pan. Mix baking mix and water; beat vigorously 20 strokes. Turn onto floured surface. Knead about 60 times or until no longer sticky. Press into 13" circle on cookie sheet; pinch edge, forming 1/2" rim, or press in pizza pan.

Mix chicken and salsa. Sprinkle crust with 1 cup of the cheese. Top with onion, chicken mixture and pepper; sprinkle with remaining cheese. Bake 12-15 or until crust is brown and cheese is bubbly.

Makes 1 pizza.

Quick Spanish Rice And Pork Chops

Ingredients:

4 Boneless Pork Chops

1/2 ts Kitchen Bouquet

4 sl Onion

2/3 c Quick Cooking Rice

1 2/3 c Pasta sauce with

Mushrooms

1/2 c Water

1/2 c Mozzarella, shredded

Directions:

NOTE: Cooking times are based on using a 625-750 watt microwave oven and food quantities for 4 servings. Adjust cooking times as required. Brush both sides of the pork chops with Kitchen Bouquet. Arrange in a single layer in a microwave safe (8" square) baking dish. Top each chop with a slice of onion. Cover with well vented plastic wrap. Microwave on high for 7 minutes. Turn the chops. Add the rice. Combine the pasta sauce and the water. Spoon over the chops. Recover with well vented plastic wrap. Microwave on high for 5 minutes. Microwave on medium (50%) until chops are tender (about 7 minutes). Sprinkle with the mozzarella. Let stand, uncovered, until the cheese melts (about 5 minutes).

Quick Sticky Buns

Ingredients:

Buns:

1/4 c Butter

1/4 c Sugar

2 pk Yeast

Topping:

1 1/2 ts Cinnamon

2 tb Corn syrup

1 1/4 c Milk

3 1/4 c Flour

1 ts Salt

1 ea Egg

1 c Brown sugar

3/4 c Butter

1 c Walnuts

Directions:

Heat milk and butter to 120 to 130 degrees. Mix together 2 cups flour, sugar, salt, yeast and egg. Add liquid and beat medium four minutes. Stir in rest of flour. Cover and rise until double (30 to 45 minutes). Generously grease 24 muffin cups. Chop nuts. Heat all topping ingredients on low until ingredients are melted and combined. Divide topping between muffin cups. Stir down batter. Drop into muffin cups. Cover and rise until double (20 to 30 minutes). Preheat oven to 375 degrees. Place tins on cookie sheet and bake 12 to 15 minutes until golden brown. Cool three minutes then invert on waxed paper.

Quick Tetrazzini

Ingredients:

1/2 lb Thin spaghetti

10 1/2 oz Condensed cream of mushroom

2 oz Mushrooms; sliced, canned

1 c Light cream; or

1 c -canned milk

2 cn Tuna; drained, flaked

1 c Soft bread crumbs

1/4 c Parmesan cheese; grated

2 tb Butter; melted

Directions:

Break spaghetti into small pieces (2 to 3 inches) and cook according to package directions. Meanwhile, combine soup, mushrooms, cream, and tuna. Drain spaghetti and combine with mushroom-tuna mixture. Put into greased 2 to 2 1/2 quart casserole. Mix bread crumbs, cheese, and melted butter and sprinkle on top of mixture in casserole. Bake in hot oven (400F) 45 minutes to 1 hour or until browned and bubbly.

Quick-fix Steak And Lemon-pepper Potatoes

Ingredients:

1 c Prepared Italian dressing

2 tb Soy sauce

1 1/2 lb Flank steak

1 1/3 lb (4 medium) potatoes cut into 2-inch chunks

1 1/2 tb Butter or margarine cut into small pieces

1 1/2 tb Fresh lemon juice

1 ts Minced garlic

1 tb Chopped parsley

1 1/2 ts Grated lemon peel

1/4 ts -to 1/2 ts Pepper

Salt, to taste

Directions:

In shallow dish or pan mix together dressing and soy sauce. Add steak, turning to coat; cover and refrigerate at least 20 minutes. Meanwhile, place potatoes, butter, lemon juice and garlic in shallow 1 1/2- to 2-quart microwave-safe dish; toss. Cover with plastic wrap, venting one corner. Microwave on HIGH 12 to 16 minutes until just tender. Meanwhile, heat broiler 10 minutes. Remove steak from marinade. Broil 4 to 5 inches from heat source 5 to 10 minutes on each side to desired doneness. While steak cooks, mix parsley, lemon peel and pepper into cooked potatoes. Season with salt and microwave on HIGH about 1 minute until hot. Slice meat diagonally across the grain into thin slices. Serve with potatoes.

So Easy Banana Caramel Pie

Ingredients:

1 Baked 8" pie shell

1/4 c Cold water

2 Egg yolks

1/2 c Granulated sugar

1/2 c Brown sugar, packed

1/4 c All-purpose flour

1/4 ts Salt

1 c Boiling water

1 tb Butter or

1/2 ts Vanilla extract

3 Or 4 ripe bananas

1/2 c Heavy cream

Directions:

Early in day: In saucepan, mix cold water with egg yolks; stir in combined sugars, flour, and salt. Gradually add boiling water, stirring briskly. Cook, stirring, 3 to 5 min., or until smooth and thick. Add butter and vanilla; cool 5 min., stirring occasionally. Pour into baked pie shell. Refrigerate till serving time.

To serve: Slice bananas over filling. Whip cream; spread over all.

Sue McNair

Super-easy Roasted Potatoes

Ingredients:

Potatoes

Oil

Onion soup mix powder

Directions:

Mix one packet of onion soup mix with some oil. Cook the same as Roasted Cajun Potatoes. [Preheat an oven to 400. Mix everything well in a roasting pan, making sure that the potatoes are coated with the oil and spices. Roast the potatoes in the oven for 45 minutes, stirring around every 15 minutes.]

Super-easy Scoreboard Dip

Ingredients:

1 pk Garlic & herb salad dressing mix

1/2 c Milk

3/4 c Mayonnaise

Directions:

Blend together all ingredients. Chill at least one hour before serving. Serve with potato chips.

Sweet And Sour Beef

Ingredients:

1 lb Lean ground beef

1 sm Onion; thinly sliced

2 ts Minced fresh ginger

1 pk 16 oz frozen mixed veggies (snap peas, carrots, water chestnuts, pineapple and red pepper)

6 tb Bottled sweet and sour sauce

Cooked rice

Directions:

Place meat, onion and ginger in large skillet; cook over high heat 6 to 8 minutes or until no longer pink, breaking meat apart with wooden spoon. Pour off drippings.

Stir in frozen vegetables and sauce. Cook, covered, 6 to 8 minutes or until vegetables are heated through. Serve over rice.

Very Quick Apple Squares

Ingredients:

3/4 c Softened butter or margarine

1 pk White cake mix

1 (21 oz.) can apple pie filling

1/2 c Flaked coconut

Directions:

In a large bowl, cut butter into dry cake mix. Set aside one cup. Press remaining mixture into 13x9 inch baking pan. Spoon pie filling evenly over cake mixture.

In a small bowl, combine reserved cake mixture and coconut. Sprinkle over pie filling. Bake at 350 degrees for 45 minutes or until golden brown. Cool slightly before cutting in 3 x 1 1/2 inch bars.

Quick Bacon Rolls

Ingredients:

1 lb. bacon

1 can water chestnuts, whole

1/2 c. ketchup

1/2 c. sugar

1/2 c. brown sugar

Toothpicks

Directions:

Preheat oven to 375 degrees. Cut bacon strips in thirds. Cut water chestnuts in half. Wrap each bacon piece around a water chestnut. Secure with a toothpick. Bake for 20 minutes or until bacon starts to crisp. Drain grease. Combine ketchup and sugars. Pour over bacon rolls and continue baking for 15-20 minutes. This is a quick, easy recipe that always gets many compliments.

Quick And Easy Meatloaf

Ingredients:

1 (10 1/2 oz.) can Campbell's cream of

mushroom soup

2 lbs. ground beef

1 pouch Campbell's dry onion soup &

recipe mix

1/2 c. dry bread crumbs

1 egg, beaten

1/4 c. water

Directions:

In large bowl, mix thoroughly 1/2 cup of the mushroom soup, beef, onion soup mix, bread crumbs and egg. In 12"x8" baking pan, firmly shape meat mixture into 8"x4" loaf. 2. Bake at 350 degrees for 1 1/4 hours or until done. Spoon off 2 tablespoons drippings; reserve. 3. In saucepan over medium heat, heat remaining soup, water and reserved drippings to boiling, stirring occasionally. Thin sauce with additional wafer to desired consistency. Spoon over meat loaf. Makes 8 servings. Prep Time 5 minutes. Cook Time 1 1/2 hours.

Quick And Easy Fish Fillets

Ingredients:

Fish fillets (1/4 to 1/2 inch thick)

Egg wash (2 eggs beaten with 1/4 c. milk)

Cracker crumbs

Peanut oil or vegetable oil for frying

Salt to taste

Directions:

Rinse fillets in cold water, drain, pat dry with paper towels. Dip fillets in egg wash. Coat with crumbs and place in a single layer on wax paper. Heat oil to 370-375 degrees. Put fillets in oil a few at a time (do not overload cooker!). As fish float to the top, cook about 30 seconds, turn, cook 30 seconds more, remove with a slotted spoon. Place on a rack.

Allow to drain and check to insure they are done (fillets will break cleanly and flake easily when done). Salt to taste. Remove from rack and place in single layers on paper towels.

Hamburger Stroganoff-Quick And Economical

Ingredients:

1 lb. ground beef

1/2 c. chopped onion

1/4 c. margarine

2 tbsp. flour

1 tsp. garlic salt

1/4 tsp. pepper

1 can cream of chicken soup

1 c. dairy sour cream

2 c. hot cooked noodles

8 oz. mushroom pieces (optional)

Directions:

In large skillet, brown ground beef. Drain off most of fat. Stir in onions and margarine and continue browning until onion is tender. Stir in flour, garlic salt, pepper, and mushrooms. Cook 5 minutes, stirring constantly. Remove from heat. Stir in soup. Simmer uncovered 10 minutes. Stir in sour cream. Heat through. Serve over noodles. Serves 6.

DEEP DISH PIZZA - QUICK!

Ingredients:

1 pkg. active dry yeast

1 c. warm water (105 to 115 degrees)

1 tsp. sugar

1 tsp. salt

2 tbsp. vegetable oil

2 1/2 c. all-purpose flour

1 (8 oz.) can pizza sauce

Toppings of choice (pepperoni,

sausage, black olives, etc.)

Mozzarella cheese

Directions:

Dissolve yeast in warm water. Stir in remaining 4 ingredients, beat with a fork 25 strokes. Let stand 5 minutes. Press dough evenly in greased deep dish pizza pan and up the sides about half way. Spread with pizza sauce and toppings. Bake at 425 degrees for 20 to 25 minutes.

Quick And Easy Barbecue Pork Chops

Ingredients:

4-5 pork chops

1/2 onion

1-2 carrots

1 stalk celery

About 1/4 c. ketchup

2-3 drops Worcestershire sauce

Water to cover chops

Directions:

Lightly brown pork chops on both sides. Put ketchup on top of pork chops. Add water to cover chops. Add onion, celery, carrots and Worcestershire sauce. Cook about 1/2 hour. This recipe can be used with beef or chicken.

QUICK LEMON PIE

Ingredients:

1 sm. can frozen lemonade

1 can Eagle brand sweetened milk

1 lg. carton Cool Whip

1 ready to serve graham cracker pie

crust

Directions:

Mix lemonade and milk; let stand a few minutes. Fold in Cool Whip. Pour into prepared graham cracker crust. Chill for 1 hour and serve.